FRANK LLOYD WRIGHT

FRANK LLOYD WRIGHT

ODYSSEYS

JENNIFER FANDEL

CREATIVE EDUCATION · CREATIVE PAPERBACKS

Published by Creative Education and Creative Paperbacks
P.O. Box 227, Mankato, Minnesota 56002
Creative Education and Creative Paperbacks are imprints of
The Creative Company
www.thecreativecompany.us

Book design by Blue Design (www.bluedes.com)
Art direction by Rita Marshall
Printed in China

Photographs by Corbis (Niall Benvie, Bettmann, Sandy Felsenthal, Michael
Freeman, Farrell Grehan, Thomas A. Heinz, John Swope Collection, Catherine
Karnow, Layne Kennedy, Marvin Koner, Charles & Josette Lenars, Gail Mooney,
Benjamin Rondel, Bob Rowan, Progressive Image, G.E. Kidder Smith, Richard
Hamilton Smith, Roger Wood), Getty Images (Alfred Eisenstaedt/Time Life
Pictures, Joe Munroe)

Writings of Frank Lloyd Wright are copyright © 2005 The Frank Lloyd Wright
Foundation, Taliesin West, Scottsdale, AZ. Used with permission.

Library of Congress Cataloging-in-Publication Data
Fandel, Jennifer.
Frank Lloyd Wright / Jennifer Fandel.
p. cm. — (Odysseys in artistry)
Includes bibliographical references and index.
Summary: A biography of American architect Frank Lloyd Wright, examining
his design influence and development of the Prairie School style, as well as
some of his most famous structures.

ISBN 978-1-60818-718-8 (hardcover)
ISBN 978-1-62832-314-6 (pbk)
ISBN 978-1-56660-754-4 (eBook)
1. Wright, Frank Lloyd, 1867–1959—Juvenile literature. 2. Architects—United
States—Biography—Juvenile literature.

NA737.W7 F285 2016
720.92—dc23   2015048529

CCSS: RI.8.1, 2, 3, 4; RI.9-10.1, 2, 3, 4; RI.11-12.1, 2, 3, 4; RH.6-8.1, 4, 5, 7;
RH.9-10.1, 3, 4

First Edition HC 9 8 7 6 5 4 3 2 1
First Edition PBK 9 8 7 6 5 4 3 2 1

CONTENTS

Finding His Way

Throughout his life, Frank Lloyd Wright was fond of saying, "Early in life, I had to choose between honest arrogance and hypocritical humility. I chose honest arrogance and have seen no occasion to change." While the American architect's boastful nature and love of the spotlight helped him cultivate a legendary status, his buildings remain a true testimony to his genius. From foundation to

OPPOSITE: Countless architects have been inspired by Frank Lloyd Wright—through his fellowship, his buildings, and the legend that he has become.

ceiling, each structure captivates the imagination, em-
bodying Wright's skillful union of modern materials and
a nature-inspired design. Considered America's finest
architect and one of the greatest 20th-century design-
ers in the world, Frank Lloyd Wright looked beyond
the building styles of the past and designed the future.

Frank Lloyd Wright was born on June 8, 1867, in
Richland Center, Wisconsin, amidst rolling hills and
fertile farmlands in the southern part of the state. His
mother, Anna Lloyd Jones, was a teacher whose family
had emigrated from Wales to Wisconsin in the 1840s.
The Lloyd Joneses were a large, tight-knit, and prosper-
ous family that valued education and held fast to their
Welsh roots and Unitarian religious background.

Frank's father, William Wright, was a minister from
the East Coast who had been educated in both medicine

and law. A gifted musician and charming speaker, William easily drew attention to himself. His amiable personality opened doors for him, and he was constantly offered new jobs—as a pastor, lecturer, musician, and lawyer. In his restlessness, he moved his family with each opportunity that came along.

Frank was the oldest of Anna and William's three children, and Anna claimed to have foreseen her son's career in architecture before he was born. Destiny was a recurring theme in the Welsh legends that Anna's family cherished, and it played an important part in how she saw the world. To help Frank toward his "calling," Anna hung drawings of English chapels around his crib. Once he reached the age of seven, she introduced him to the Froebel method, a visual education technique involving wooden building blocks and colorful paper shapes.

From this, Frank learned to see geometry and forms in nature—from the complex root system in trees to the pattern of petals on a flower.

Throughout Frank's childhood, his family moved around the East and Midwest. By the time they settled down in Wisconsin's capital city of Madison, 11-year-old Frank had lived in 6 different towns across 4 states. A shy boy, Frank enjoyed reading novels, playing the piano and viola, and painting. Preferring his own private world to interaction with his family or fellow classmates, Frank found sanctuary in his bedroom as a teenager. The warnings "Sanctum Sanctorum" (Latin for "Sacred Sanctuary") and "Keep Out" graced a sign outside his bedroom door. Inside the bedroom, nature scenes that he had painted decorated the walls.

While Frank's mother nurtured her son's artistic inclinations and held fast to her early visions of his architect future, she worried about his behavior as he grew older. When he did leave the security of his bedroom, he seemed intent to dress and act the part of a fashionable dandy—wearing such showy items as a stovepipe hat—instead of presenting himself as a young man of substance. He had difficulty fitting in among his peers, as he rarely dropped the romantic guises he had dreamed up for himself.

OPPOSITE Although he did not enjoy the work, summers on his uncle's farm in Wisconsin gave Wright the opportunity to experience the natural world.

Hoping to toughen him up and shake him from his dreamy tendencies, Frank's parents sent him to work each summer on his uncle James Lloyd Jones's farm in Spring Green, a rural town a short distance from Madison. The farm's physical labor and grueling schedule, which included rising at 4:00 A.M. to milk cows, was completely foreign to Frank. Accustomed to the comforts of town life, the teenager was also shocked by the constant amount of work required to run a farm, from tending livestock to chopping firewood and harvesting crops. He despised the work and even tried running away on more than one occasion.

Despite his dislike for farm work, Frank fell in love with the land that surrounded him. Steep hillsides were broken by jagged limestone outcroppings, and

"His intimacy with nature enabled him to translate it into architectural terms. In the patterns of nature, the formation of a snowflake ... the indentations and lines in a jagged rock hanging over the sea, it was an inner beat, an inner rhythm he listened to ... bringing never-ending variety into architecture."

— Olgivanna Wright, Frank's third wife

the Wisconsin River curved through the valley below. Even when he ran away from the farm, he never went far, finding a comfortable hay bale on which to rest or discovering a new bluff from which to sit and think.

Surrounded by his stalwart uncle and cousins, Frank was left little opportunity for idle dreaming, however. Whenever he was caught slacking, Uncle James recited his favorite adage, "Add tired to tired, and then add it again." The teenager grew annoyed hearing it repeated so often, but it made a lasting impression on him. As an adult, Frank would reflect happily on the phrase and on those summers on the farm. No matter how enormous the task or how daunting the obstacle he faced, the saying reminded Frank that a strong will and hard work could take him to a better future.

The Right Angle

In 1885, before he turned 18, Frank suddenly found himself on his own. His parents divorced, and he would never again see his father. Quitting his last year of high school, Frank found work as a junior **draftsman** for a civil engineer at the University of Wisconsin in Madison and enrolled for two semesters of college courses there. Frank's mother expected him to take his father's place and support the family, but Frank hated to be practical with his money. He spent most of his

OPPOSITE: Frank's training as a draftsman helped him sketch out projects and envision structural designs that would inform his later architectural work.

paychecks on extravagant clothes, books, and trips to the theater—anything to show that he was a man of possibility, class, and style.

While at the university, Frank got his first taste of architectural design work. His uncle Jenkin Lloyd Jones had commissioned Chicago architect Joseph Lyman Silsbee to design a chapel near Spring Green, and Frank was allowed to assist in the interior design, becoming known in family circles as "the boy architect." In 1887, Frank moved to Chicago, taking a draftsman's position at Sils-bee's firm. That year, Frank's schoolteacher aunts asked him to design a building for their school, Hillside, near Spring Green. This was his first building design to be executed, and Frank suddenly saw his future. He began signing his drawings "Frank Lloyd Wright, Architect." After only one year under Silsbee, Frank was hired at Adler and Sullivan, one of Chicago's most prestigious and cutting-edge architectural firms.

In 1889, Frank married Catherine Tobin, an intel-ligent and spirited woman from a well-to-do Unitarian family. Frank was 21, and Catherine was 18. Already in Louis Sullivan's good favor, Frank asked him for a loan to build a home in Oak Park, a developing suburb of Chicago. In 1890, the first of Frank and Catherine's six children was born.

Sullivan immediately recognized Frank's immense talent; by the age of 22, Frank was the company's chief designer and was supervising 30 draftsmen. Wealthy clients occasionally approached the firm with requests for residential designs. These projects were an inconvenience to Sullivan, who preferred high-profit commercial designs, but they were the jobs Frank wanted. As his reputation for residential design spread, Frank began moonlighting after hours, designing houses around Chicago and its suburbs. This was against the firm's policy, and when confronted about his freelance work, Frank quit, confident of making his own opportunities.

In 1893, when he was 26, Frank went into private practice. He developed what he called Prairie Style homes—stone and wood homes with an open floor plan,

OPPOSITE The influence of both nature and geometry can be seen in much of Wright's work, including the triangular-shaped pool at Taliesin West.

a center fireplace, and walls of endless windows to let in natural light. For Frank, this wasn't a passing style but the groundwork for his theory of organic architecture. His concept had its roots in Louis Sullivan's theory of "Form Follows Function." Before Sullivan, architects thought little of a building's practical use and simply reused the styles of past ages. Sullivan had helped launch architecture into the modern era by proposing that the design of a building impact its purpose. But Frank took Sullivan's theory a step farther, insisting on a design employing absolute harmony among the land, the materials, the building's function, and its occupants. He expressed this theory with the phrase "Form and Function Are One."

In his first year of private practice, Frank received five commissions, or orders, for residential designs. For the next seven years, he had more than enough work,

"Some of these [houses] seem to grow out of the ground as naturally as the trees, and to express our hospitable suburban American life, a life of indoors and outdoors, as spontaneously as certain Italian villas express the more pompous and splendid life of those old gorgeous centuries."

— American writer Harriet Monroe, commenting on Wright's work at a 1907 exhibition

Wright's distinctive hat and cane continued to be hallmarks of his ensemble as he aged.

with up to nine commissions a year. An excellent self-promoter, he published articles, gave speeches, and exhibited models and designs, including a solo exhibit in 1907 at the Art Institute of Chicago. Although many of his wealthy and often conservative clients thought his designs a bit too adventurous, Frank relied on the traits he had inherited from his father—charm, humor, and a way with words—to talk them into approving his plans.

The citizens of Chicago soon came to recognize the man with the broad-brimmed hat whose hair grew slightly over his collar. Frank often wore a dramatic cape and carried a cane, which he used to gesture grandly and accentuate the importance of his ideas. From 1900 on, his name would be a constant feature in the newspapers. And publicity, good or bad, was something that Frank never seemed to mind.

Breaking Boundaries

Between 1894 and 1911, Frank designed 135 buildings throughout the United States, focusing most of his efforts on residential design. Yet in spite of his success, he grew unhappy toward the end of this period. Not yet 40 years old, Frank felt restless: he found domestic life in Oak Park oppressive, and his work no longer held the spark of his earlier years. To escape his dissatisfaction, he

OPPOSITE: Oak Park, Illinois, boasts many buildings designed by Wright, including his first home, which he built with $5,000 borrowed from Louis Sullivan.

abandoned his family and traveled to Europe with Mamah Cheney, the wife of a client. From 1909 to 1910, Frank lived in Berlin, Germany, and Florence, Italy, while working on the first foreign publication of his designs.

When he returned to Oak Park, Frank's residential design opportunities had largely vanished. Most of his clients found his behavior deplorable, and the newspapers' coverage of the scandal had marred his reputation far beyond Chicago. It was then, having recently inherited land in

Spring Green, that Frank began building his artistic re-treat and eventual home, Taliesin. In 1911, when Frank and Mamah moved into Taliesin, the gossip about their lives still hadn't subsided. Frank explained himself by saying, "The ordinary man cannot live without rules to guide his conduct. It is infinitely more difficult to live without rules, but that is what the really honest, sincere, thinking man is compelled to do."

Around this time, Frank received a number of com-missions for commercial structures. One of his most striking designs was a beer garden, restaurant, and dance hall complex in Chicago called Midway Gardens. In 1914, while he was working on the project, tragedy struck at Taliesin. A crazed servant killed Mamah, her two children, and four visitors and set fire to the home. Some viewed the event as punishment for Frank's immoral behavior, and many wondered if the misfortune would spell the end of his career. Despite Frank's immense sorrow, quitting was not an option to him. The only part of his home that survived the fire was his studio, and Frank took it as a sign: he would rebuild Taliesin and continue his work.

Nearly two years later, in 1916, Frank gained a foothold in international design with his $4.5-million commission for the new Imperial Hotel in Tokyo, Japan. After experiencing an earthquake in Japan, he designed

the building in flexible sections that could expand and contract in a tremor. In 1923, a year after the Imperial Hotel was completed, one of the largest earthquakes of the 20th century struck Tokyo. Not only did the building hold up with only slight damage, but it was so structurally sound that it became a shelter for earthquake refugees.

During the six years it took to build the hotel, Frank spent most of his time in Japan, a country whose design principles of simplicity and harmony with nature appealed to him immensely. During these years, he found companionship with an American woman named Miriam Noel. Their relationship was a rocky one that lasted nine years. In 1923, they married, but Miriam left him after only six months.

In late 1924, Frank met Olgivanna Lazovich Hinzenberg, a young Montenegrin dancer and intellectual, at a ballet performance in Chicago. She was 26, and he was 57. They immediately fell in love and had a baby, a daughter named Iovanna, in late 1925. In all of his relationships, Frank's personality traits—his self-centeredness, mercurialness, and obsession with work—had made life difficult for spouses and companions. Although he changed little, Frank found a matching artistic spirit and a selfless companion in Olgivanna. They were married in 1928.

In the late 1920s and early '30s, the Great Depression froze most design projects in America. To ensure a steady income for his family, Frank wrote and lectured around the world on his design philosophies. He and Olgivanna also began a fellowship program at Taliesin. Through the program, talented young architects would learn the art of organic architecture through design work and labor on the Wrights' self-sustaining farm. Frank's reputation attracted immediate recruits, and the Taliesin Fellowship quickly became famous internationally.

With his new team of fellowship assistants ("the fingers of my hand," as Frank referred to them), Frank was able to take on more design work, and he came out of the Depression with ideas enough to redesign the world. In interviews and casual conversations, when asked to name his masterpiece, Frank always replied, "The next one." In the beginning of 1943, he had no idea how true his words would turn out to be.

A Triumphant Design

On October 21, 1959, upper 5th Avenue in Manhattan was buzzing with activity. Men in sharp suits and women in fitted dresses spilled down the block, waiting to enter Frank Lloyd Wright's crowning achievement, a museum of modern and contemporary art called the Solomon R. Guggenheim Museum. Referred to by Frank as an "inverted **ziggurat**," the curved white structure astonished the crowd.

OPPOSITE: With the Guggenheim, Wright broke up the rectangular-shaped grid prevalent in New York, a city he considered overbuilt and overpopulated.

39

The wonder of that day had actually been set in motion 16 years earlier, when Frank received his commission for the project in a letter from the museum's curator, Hilla Rebay. In that 1943 letter, she told him of her grandiose expectations for the project, exclaiming, "I need a fighter, a lover of space, an agitator, a tester and a wise man.... I want a temple of spirit, a monument!" Frank knew he was the man to deliver such a building.

Despite Frank's enthusiasm, the project took more than a decade and a half. In the summer of 1943, Frank and the project's benefactor, Solomon R. Guggenheim, a multimillionaire who made his fortune in mining, signed the design contracts. In a letter to Rebay, Frank expressed how urgent the project was to him. He wrote, "I am so full of ideas for our museum that I am likely to blow up or commit suicide unless I can let them out on paper." In

1944, once the building site was selected, Frank began the process of drawing and revising his ideas, making more than 100 sketches.

n 1946, Frank revealed his vision of the building with a cutaway model of its exterior and interior. Over the next 10 years, he confronted skeptical city commissioners in an effort to get a building permit for his innovative structure. In the end, Frank told his Taliesin apprentices, he designed the building to please no one but himself. In 1956, groundbreaking ceremonies took place, and the construction finally began.

Starting in August 1956, New Yorkers watched with curiosity and awe as an odd-shaped structure grew out of molded concrete and reinforced steel from the plot of cleared land. Among the boxy, monotone high-rises of 5th Avenue across from Central Park, the Guggenheim Museum emerged as an eye-catching white building that broke up the skyline with its sweeping curves and inverted cone design.

Even more striking than the exterior was the marriage of form and function inside the building. Most previous museums were designed in square grids that required their patrons to cross through previously seen exhibit halls in order to enter another wing. Frank was sure he could avoid this traditional, and often tiresome, design. Carrying the curves of the outside structure to the inside of the building, he designed a gradual ramp that led patrons from exhibit to exhibit seamlessly after riding an elevator to the top. It was as if one floor flowed into the next. From any position on the ramp, viewers could see the evolution of an artist's career, and, looking toward the building's center, they could see the museum's collection as a whole. In addition, Frank incorporated natural lighting with a large circular skylight and lowered the ceiling height to create a greater sense of intimacy with the art and the museum space.

Further reflecting nature, the interior of the museum suggests the spiral of a nautilus shell, with one space moving freely into the next.

As was common of Frank's work, his radical design drew considerable fire from critics. When artists complained that his building would overshadow the art housed in the museum, Frank wrote, "On the contrary, [the museum was designed] to make the building and the painting an uninterrupted, beautiful symphony such as never existed in the World of Art before."

While touring the museum on its opening day, the nearly 3,000 patrons remarked little on the works by Wassily Kandinsky, Marc Chagall, Paul Klee, and Pablo Picasso. Instead, they focused on the spaces they were walking through, taking in the breathtaking white curves. Olgivanna affectionately termed the museum Frank's "Miracle on 5th Avenue," and those words seemed fitting for that October day. Most of the patrons—art aficionados, architecture buffs, and curious citizens alike—had only read about the experience of Frank Lloyd Wright's modern designs, and they were dazzled by what they saw. In their eyes, the Guggenheim was not just a building; it was a marvel—a masterpiece—that rose from the street.

Love of an Idea

In 1930, at an age when many of his colleagues were contemplating the ease of retirement, 63-year-old Frank hit a new stride, producing some of the most creative and noteworthy designs of his career. In the realm of residential design was Frank's 1935 masterpiece Fallingwater, built in Pennsylvania for Edgar J. Kaufmann Sr., a wealthy Pittsburgh department store owner. Kaufmann's family wanted a home with views of their

OPPOSITE: After viewing the waterfall, Wright wrote to Edgar Kaufmann that Fallingwater was taking shape in his mind "to the music of the stream."

favorite waterfall. Frank responded by anchoring the house's foundation into the waterfall's rock ledges, creating a structure that was one with the nature that surrounded it.

A year later, Frank designed a stunning commercial structure, the S. C. Johnson and Son Administration Building in Racine, Wisconsin. Striving to infuse the American workplace with artistry and a connection to nature, Frank designed glass tube walkways and skylights that let an abundance of natural light into the building. The centerpiece of his design was an open workspace filled with lily pad-shaped columns made of steel-enforced concrete and covered with Pyrex, a shiny, heat-resistant glass.

By 1937, Frank and his family—Olgivanna, their daughter Iovanna, and his adopted daughter Svetlana—were spending their winters at Taliesin West, a desert retreat near Scottsdale, Arizona. After Frank suffered a serious bout of pneumonia in 1936, his doctor had encouraged him to move to a milder climate during the winter months. The following year, 70-year-old Frank built Taliesin West, a stunning collection of buildings constructed of redwood and concrete mixed with bright desert stones.

Besides design commissions, Frank received many awards and honors in the last 30 years of his life. In 1949, at the age of 81, he was awarded the Gold Medal from the American Institute of Architecture, an award that

the institute had bestowed on less talented (according to Frank) architects in prior years. To make his simultaneous pleasure and displeasure known, Frank began his acceptance speech by saying, "Well, it's about time." In addition to this major award, he received honorary doctorates from Princeton and the University of Wisconsin. Also, to commemorate his achievements on an annual basis, both Chicago and Spring Green began celebrating a "Frank Lloyd Wright Day."

In 1957, Frank received 40 commissions, a record for his career. The work was showing no sign of letting up, and neither was the 90-year-old architect. While he let his Taliesin assistants take on more of the drawing work, Frank was awake early every morning "playing" with his T-square, triangle, and compass, working out new designs. Between the ages of 75 and 91, he designed more than 500 projects—more than half of the design work that he produced throughout his 70-year career. Of his total designs, he lived to see 532 structures completed.

Although Frank spent much of his later years working, he seldom turned down an interview or speaking engagement. In one national television interview, the notoriously outspoken architect boasted, "Having now had the experience [of building] 769 buildings, it's quite easy for me to shake them out of my sleeve. It's amazing what I could do for this country." At other times, however, Frank became deeply reflective about his architectural legacy. In a speech toward the end of his life, he said, "I do not consider myself a success. I feel, rather, that I am a brilliant failure, because as yet the United States has no organic architecture."

Only months away from his 92nd birthday, Frank

was energetic and in good health. Then, one night in early April 1959, he was rushed to the hospital with severe stomach pains. After a successful operation for an intestinal blockage, Frank looked to be on his way to a full recovery. But on April 9, in a hospital in Phoenix, Arizona, he quietly passed away.

Frank's Taliesin apprentices drove their teacher's body back to his beloved Wisconsin to be buried. On the day of the funeral, more than 200 mourners walked behind a horse and cart carrying Frank's flower-draped coffin. They walked through the lands that had nourished and inspired him, stopping at his resting place in the family graveyard. "Love of an idea is love of God" is all that his simple stone said.

In His Words

Frank Lloyd Wright was a prolific writer and lecturer on his theories and philosophy of architectural design. The following excerpts, taken from works published in 1909, 1914, and 1931, show the development of Wright's ideas on organic architecture, from his middle years to his later years as an elder architect speaking to his followers.

The following excerpt is from *Ausgeführte Bauten und Entwürfe von Frank Lloyd Wright* (Completed

OPPOSITE: The Marin County Civic Center in California was Wright's 770th commission and his final work, which he did not live to see completed.

Buildings and Designs by Frank Lloyd Wright). Published in Berlin, Germany, in 1909, this was Wright's first book-length publication.

In America each man has a peculiar, inalienable right to live in his own house in his own way. He is a pioneer in every right sense of the word. His home environment may face forward, may portray his character, tastes, and ideas, if he has any, and every man here has some somewhere about him.

This is a condition at which Englishmen or Europeans, facing toward traditional forms which they are in duty bound to preserve, may well stand aghast. An American is in duty bound to establish traditions in harmony with his ideals, his still unspoiled sites, his industrial opportunities, and industrially he is more completely committed to the

"Mr. Wright was a 'practical visionary.' He could talk about architectural ideas and about pouring a concrete wall and make all of it sound equally real and equally important. He loved the luxuries, but also as a kind of balance he appreciated the hardships, welcomed a chance to overcome them."

— **John Rattenbury, a Taliesin Fellowship apprentice**

machine than any living man. It has given him the things which mean mastery over an uncivilized land—comfort and resources.

H is machine, the tool in which his opportunity lies, can only murder the traditional forms of other peoples and earlier times. He must find new forms, new industrial ideals, or stultify both opportunity and forms. But underneath forms in all ages were certain conditions which determined them. In them all was a human spirit in accord with which they came to be; and

FRANK LLOYD WRIGHT

where the forms were true forms, they will be found to be organic forms—an outgrowth, in other words, of conditions of life and work they arose to express. They are beautiful and significant, studied in this relation. They are dead to us, borrowed as they stand.

I have called this feeling for the organic character of form and treatment the Gothic spirit, for it was more completely realized in the forms of that architecture, perhaps, than any other. At least the infinitely varied forms of that architecture are more obviously and literally organic than any other, and the spirit in which they were conceived and wrought was one of absolute integrity of means to ends. In this spirit America will find the forms best suited to her opportunities, her aims, and her life.

All the great styles, approached from within, are spiritual treasure houses to architects. Transplanted as

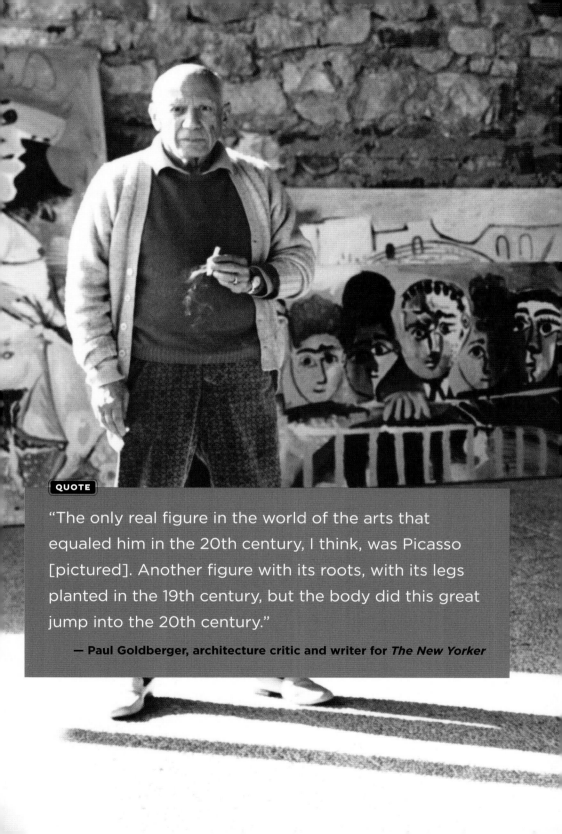

"The only real figure in the world of the arts that equaled him in the 20th century, I think, was Picasso [pictured]. Another figure with its roots, with its legs planted in the 19th century, but the body did this great jump into the 20th century."

— Paul Goldberger, architecture critic and writer for *The New Yorker*

forms, they are tombs of a life that has been lived.

The following excerpt is from "Taliesin," an article published in *The Architectural Record* in May 1914. "Romeo and Juliet" in the article refers to a windmill that Wright designed.

Taliesin was the name of a Welsh Poet. A druid-bard or singer of songs who sang to Wales the glories of Fine Art. Literally the Welsh word means "shining brow." Many legends cling to the name in Wales....

This hill on which Taliesin now stands as "brow" was one of my favorite places when I was a boy, for pasque flowers grew there in March sun while snow still streaked the hillsides.

When you are on its crown you are out in mid-air as

though swinging in a plane, as the valley and two others drop away leaving the tree-tops all about you. "Romeo and Juliet" stands in plain view to the southeast, the Hillside Home School just over the ridge.

As "the boy" I had learned the ground-plan of the region in every line and feature. Its "elevation" for me now is the modelling of the hills, the weaving and the fabric that clings to them, the look of it all in tender green or covered with snow or in full glow of summer that bursts into the glorious blaze of autumn.

I still feel myself as much a part of it as the trees and birds and bees, and red barns, or as the animals are, for that matter....

Architecture, by now, was mine. It had come by actual experience to mean to me something out of the ground of what we call "America," something in league with the

stones of the field, in sympathy with "the flower that fadeth, the grass that withereth," something of the prayerful consideration for the lilies of the field that was my gentle grandmother's. Something natural to the change that was "America" herself.

And it was unthinkable … that any house should be put on that beloved hill. I knew well by now that no house should ever be on any hill or on anything. It should be of the hill, belonging to it, so hill and house could live together each the happier for the other. That was the way everything found round about was naturally managed, except when man did something. When he added his mite he became imitative and ugly. Why? Was there no natural house? I had proved, I felt, that there was, and now I, too, wanted a natural house to live in myself. I scanned the hills of the region where the rock came cropping out in strata to suggest buildings. How quiet and strong the rock-ledge masses looked with the dark red cedars and white birches, there, above the green slopes. They were all part of the countenance of southern Wisconsin.

I wished to be part of my beloved southern Wisconsin and not put my small part of it out of countenance. Architecture, after all, I have learned, or before all, I should say, is no less a weaving and a fabric than the trees. And as anyone might see, a beech tree is a beech tree. It isn't trying to be an oak. Nor is a pine trying to be a birch, although each makes the other more beautiful when seen together.

The world has had appropriate buildings before—why not more appropriate buildings now than ever before? There must be some kind of house that would belong to that hill, as trees and the ledges of rock did; as Grandfather and Mother had belonged to it, in their sense of it all.

Even the Midway Barns at Wright's Taliesin estate in rural Wisconsin reflect his belief that buildings must emerge naturally from their surroundings.

FRANK LLOYD WRIGHT

Yes, there must be a natural house, not natural as caves and log-cabins were natural but native in spirit and making, with all that architecture had meant whenever it was alive in times past. Nothing at all that I had ever seen would do. This country had changed all that into something else. Grandfather and Grandmother were something splendid in themselves that I couldn't imagine in any period houses I had ever seen. But there was a house that hill might marry and live happily with ever after. I fully intended to find it. I even saw, for myself, what it might be like and began to build it as the "brow" of the hill.

The following excerpt is from "To the Young Man in Architecture," which appeared in Wright's 1931 publication *Two Lectures in Architecture*.

Organic architecture seeks superior sense of use and a finer sense of comfort, expressed in organic simplicity. That is what you, young man, should call architecture. Use and comfort in order to become architecture must become spiritual satisfactions wherein the soul insures a more subtle use, achieves a more constant repose. So, architecture speaks as poetry to the soul. In this machine age to utter this poetry that is architecture, as in all other ages, you must learn the organic language of the natural which is ever the language of the new. To know any language you must know the alphabet. The alphabet in architecture in our machine age is the nature of steel, glass, and concrete

"Part of his greatness was the degree to which he was in touch with American life, American psychology, and to some extent, the degree to which he was in touch with the 20th century.... He understood the car. He understood the modern workplace."

— American architect Robert A. M. Stern

construction,—the nature of the machines used as tools, and the nature of the new materials to be used....

Yes, modern architecture is young architecture,—the joy of youth must bring it. The love of youth, eternal youth must develop and keep it. You must see this architecture as wise, but not so much wise as sensible and wistful,—nor any more scientific than sentient, nor so much resembling a flying machine as a masterpiece of the imagination.

Consider well that a house is a machine in which to live but architecture begins where that concept of the house ends. All life is machinery in a rudimentary sense, and yet machinery is the life of nothing. Machinery is machinery only because of life. It is better for you to proceed from the generals to the particulars. So do not rationalize from machinery to life. Why not think from life to machines?

FRANK LLOYD WRIGHT

The utensil, the weapon, the automaton—all are appliances. The song, the masterpiece, the edifice are a warm outpouring of the heart of man,—human delight in life triumphant: we glimpse the infinite.

That glimpse or vision is what makes art a matter of inner experience, therefore sacred, and no less but rather more individual in this age, I assure you, than ever before....

Eye-weary of reiterated bald commonplaces wherein light is rejected from blank surfaces or fallen dismally into holes cut in them, organic architecture brings the man once more face to face with nature's play of shade and depth of shadow seeing fresh vistas of native creative human thought and native feeling presented to his imagination for consideration. This is modern.

The sense of interior space as reality in organic architecture coordinates with the enlarged means of modern materials. The building is now found in this sense of interior space; the enclosure is no longer found in terms of mere roof or walls but as "screened" space. This reality is modern.

In true modern architecture, therefore, the sense of surface and mass disappears in light, or fabrications that combine it with strength. And this fabrication is no less the expression of principle as power-directed-toward-purpose than may be seen in any modern appliance or utensil machine. But modern architecture affirms the higher human sensibility of the sunlit space. Organic buildings are the strength and lightness of the spiders' spinning, buildings qualified by light, bred by native character to environment—married to the ground. That is modern!

Timeline

1867 Frank Lloyd Wright is born in Richland Center, Wisconsin, on June 8.

1885 Wright leaves high school; he begins studying and working at the University of Wisconsin.

1887 Wright goes to work under architect Joseph Lyman Silsbee in Chicago.

1888 Wright begins a six-year stint under renowned architect Louis Sullivan at the Chicago architectural firm Adler and Sullivan.

1889 Wright marries Catherine Tobin and designs their Oak Park, Illinois, home.

1893 Wright opens his own firm in Chicago; five years later, he expands his Oak Park home and moves his practice there.

1900 Wright designs his first Prairie Style residence.

1909 Wright moves to Berlin, Germany, with Mamah Cheney; his first foreign collection of designs is published.

1911 Wright builds Taliesin on family land in Spring Green, Wisconsin, and Mamah moves there with him.

1914 A servant murders Mamah and burns Taliesin; Wright rebuilds the next year.

1916 Wright receives the Imperial Hotel commission in Tokyo, Japan, and soon moves to Japan.

1924 Wright meets Olgivanna Lazovich Hinzenberg, and they have a daughter named Iovanna the following year. They marry four years later.

1932 Wright opens Taliesin as an architectural fellowship.

1943 Wright receives his commission for the Solomon R. Guggenheim Museum in New York.

1949 Wright is awarded the Gold Medal from the American Institute of Architecture.

1959 Wright dies in Phoenix, Arizona, two months shy of his 92nd birthday.

Selected Bibliography

Huxtable, Ada Louise. *Frank Lloyd Wright*. New York: Lipper / Viking, 2004.

Pfeiffer, Bruce Brooks, ed. *Frank Lloyd Wright Collected Writings*. Vols. 1 and 2. New York: Rizzoli, 1992.

Riley, Terence, ed. *Frank Lloyd Wright, Architect*. New York: Museum of Modern Art, 1994.

Secrest, Meryle. *Frank Lloyd Wright: A Biography*. Chicago: University of Chicago Press, 1998.

Wright, Frank Lloyd. *An Autobiography*. Petaluma, Calif.: Pomegranate, 2005.

Glossary

Adler and Sullivan a Chicago design firm that gained prominence with its visually appealing skyscrapers and other commercial structures in the late 1800s and early 1900s

draftsman a person who assists an architect, drawing what the architect designs

Great Depression a time in American history, lasting from 1929 to 1941, when the stock market crashed, businesses failed, and unemployment skyrocketed

Joseph Lyman Silsbee a Chicago architect known for his homey and intricate residential designs for the wealthy in the late 1800s and early 1900s

Louis Sullivan a late 19th- and early 20th-century American architect whose design principle of "form influences function" encouraged architects to create designs to complement a building's use

open floor plan an interior design plan that uses columns instead of walls for ceiling support, allowing rooms to flow into one another

organic architecture Wright's theory of harmony among all aspects of a building—from its residents and purpose to its materials and location

Prairie Style Wright's early residential style, which maximized connections between nature and the Midwestern lifestyle; his followers were referred to as the Prairie School

Unitarian a Christian denomination that holds as its foundation a freedom from strict religious doctrine; instead, reason, conscientiousness, religious tolerance, and goodness are stressed

ziggurat a pyramid-shaped tower that has steps leading to the top

Index